Published by:
The Sword of the Spirit © 2021
All rights reserved

This book is a celebration of 50 years of Covenant Community.

Design by: María del Mar Montero
Photos by: Jerusalem Community, Kairos RIA, Ligaya ng Panginoon Community, The Servants of the Word, Word of Life Community, Work of Christ Community, Youthworks Detroit, Youth Initiatives, Nico Angleys, Juan C. Aragón, Tom Caballes, Gastón De Mezerville, Tom Gryniewicz, Paul Jordan, David Kurani, Jeff Lansangan, Patti Mansfield Gallagher, Andy Pettman, Eugenio Regidor.
The text is adapted from "The History of the Sword of the Spirit" which was written by Bob Bell, Henry Dieterich and Bruce Yocum.
Edited by: Juan C. Aragón, Dave Hughes and Dan Keating
ISBN: 9781794294691

Contents

Dear brothers and sisters,

Fifty years ago, God began a new thing – calling into being communities of men and women, families and single people, who would covenant themselves together in lives of Christian love, service and mission. This book attempts to trace the history of that work of God and show our own small part in it. The book is a celebration and remembrance of what he has done.

The scriptures stress the importance of remembrance. When we recall what God has done in the past, our faith is strengthened, our hope is renewed, our love deepened.

I will remember the deeds
of the LORD;
yes, I will remember **YOUR
MIRACLES OF LONG AGO.**
I will consider all your works
and meditate on all your
mighty deeds.

Psalm 77:11-12

We had planned to do more as a community of communities to mark the 50th anniversary but the COVID-19 Pandemic interfered with our plans. Although we were prevented from coming together as we had wanted, our prayer is that this book will stir each of our hearts to remember and give thanks for what God has done.

Remembering what God has done in the past also prepares us for the next season of mission. We believe in fact that God is calling us to return in a deeper way to the roots of our beginnings – to renew our openness to the power of the Holy Spirit, to restore and deepen our call to ecumenism, to widen the tent pegs of our hearts for new mission and new relationships.

In all of this, may the Lord grant us the grace to be faithful in following after him, always listening for his voice.

In Christ,

Jean Barbara,
President of the Sword of the Spirit

Introduction

To proclaim the great deeds of God and to tell of his saving acts is to worship him. Recalling and recounting what God has done among us in these fifty years is, first of all, an act of worship, and we tell this story so that God might be glorified through it.

But there is more. We have a duty to proclaim these great deeds of God so that others can see the goodness of God and acknowledge him.

Proclaiming the great works of God is an incitement to faith for all who hear of them.

We also have a duty to pass on to coming generations our testimony to what God has done among us and to speak of God's goodness and mercy to our children and our children's children.

In telling the story of what God has done in our midst we also tell the story of our response to God.

As it was with the people of Israel, sometimes we respond well and other times we respond poorly.

We do not tell this story to boast, except of our own weakness and the greatness of God. In Christ, our weakness is a testimony to the power of God.

The purpose of this book is to tell in brief the story of how God has called together Christians from many churches to form an ecumenical, charismatic community of communities based in a common covenant.

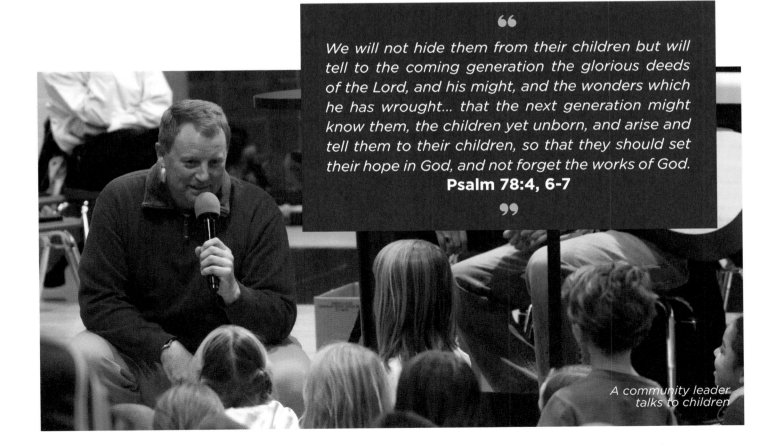

> We will not hide them from their children but will tell to the coming generation the glorious deeds of the Lord, and his might, and the wonders which he has wrought... that the next generation might know them, the children yet unborn, and arise and tell them to their children, so that they should set their hope in God, and not forget the works of God.
> **Psalm 78:4, 6-7**

A community leader talks to children

The Sword of the Spirit.

The Sword of the Spirit is part of a **larger movement of covenant communities** throughout the world, some of them joined together in networks, some standing on their own.

This movement of communities is a sign of the times, when Christians long divided from one another are coming together to seek unity and stand together for the gospel. In the face of a world grown more and more hostile to Christianity, the support of brothers and sisters in Christ is very welcome and urgently needed.

The immediate occasion for this book is the fiftieth anniversary of the initial making of a covenant in **September 1970** that bound together brothers and sisters in what has come to be known as **'covenant community'**.

This anniversary follows close upon the fiftieth anniversary of the beginning of the Charismatic Renewal in the Catholic Church which flowed out of an even larger movement of God known as the Pentecostal movement.

The Sword of the Spirit, and the larger covenant community movement of which it is a part, has its origin in and is a response to this larger movement of God.

This fiftieth anniversary is a time for looking back at what God has done in the past and for considering what he is calling us to embrace in the future.

Anecdotes from early days

A "homey" basement:
by Tom Gryniewicz
Word of Life
Ann Arbor MI, USA

One time the fire Marshall told us we'd have to stop the meetings because they were too large for the small apartment. The only place available for free was the basement of St. Mary's Student Chapel. We were afraid the meetings might not work in an "institutional setting" so we bought 2 lamps at the salvation army to try and make the huge basement seem "homey" like the apartment was. The end result was pitifully puny.

The dry bones' song:
by Gordy DeMarais
Christ the Redeemer
St. Paul MN, USA

In the early days we used to sing some funny songs. Sometimes I still wonder how I was attracted to such a thing and got involved with it. We used to sing this song called The Dry Bones from Ezekiel and, when we sang that song, people would pull keys out of their pocket and start jingling their keys during worship time.

Disastrous weekend away:
by Mimi Turner
Antioch Community
London, UK

In our first weekend away as a community in London we went to a manor house which was in the process of being renovated. The kids were sleeping in a barn out of which the cows had been moved out so the children could stay. There was only one bathroom for the whole community and no showers. We still talk about that weekend away and remember it.

PART 1
—
History of Covenant Communities

The History of the Pentecostal Movement

We begin this story with a consideration of the origin of the Catholic Charismatic Renewal, and of the larger Pentecostal movement that preceded it.

On January 1, 1901, the first day of the first year in the twentieth century, Pope Leo XIII intoned the hymn Veni Creator Spiritus (Come, Creator Spirit) in the name of the whole Catholic Church.

On the very same day, an event took place not only geographically, but also theologically, far from Rome, in a Protestant Bible college in Topeka, Kansas. It marked the beginning of a great revival in the power and gifts of the Holy Spirit destined to sweep throughout the United States and around the world. This was the dramatic beginning of the Pentecostal movement.

During the nineteenth century, many Protestant preachers and teachers in both Great Britain and the United States taught the doctrine of sanctification through an experience of a "second blessing" after conversion, sometimes referred to as a baptism in the Holy Spirit or a "baptism by fire."

The Pentecostal movement, as we now call it, began when a former Methodist preacher, Charles Fox Parham, experienced what he called a miraculous healing from a chronic condition that had prevented him from walking without crutches, and after which he became an independent evangelist in the Methodist Holiness movement, preaching "the necessity of being baptized in the Holy Spirit."

Charles Fox Parham

After attempting to found several missions, he settled in Topeka, Kansas, and founded the **Bethel Bible School** in 1898.

Parham and his students undertook a program of biblical study to determine a particular sign of the baptism in the Holy Spirit.

In December 1900, they concluded that the evidence of baptism in the Holy Spirit was speaking in tongues. Parham called for an all-night prayer service on New Year's Eve 1900, and it was during that service that he laid hands on and prayed for Agnes Ozman, one of his students, and she began to speak in what Parham said was identified as Mandarin Chinese.

*Other students came to speak in what Parham later claimed were **over twenty different languages.***

William J. Seymour

One of his students who became an influential leader in the new Pentecostal movement was an African-American named **William J. Seymour**. A small Holiness mission in Los Angeles California, invited Seymour to preach in early 1906. This congregation, comprising both black and white believers, soon outgrew their building and moved to a former African Methodist church on Azusa Street in April 1906.

The Azusa Street revival that began with Seymour's arrival in Los Angeles was the real beginning of twentieth-century Pentecostalism as a movement.

The revival attracted both positive and negative attention. Their meetings drew many pastors, evangelists and missionaries. Many of these visitors took the Pentecostal message home to other parts of the United States and abroad.

A similar but independent revival occurred in Wales in 1904, led by a young preacher named Evan Roberts. This revival incorporated many of the manifestations found in Pentecostalism, including ecstatic singing and dancing, people falling down under the influence of the Holy Spirit, and extended periods of group prayer.

In the late 1960s, several Orthodox priests from various jurisdictions in North America were active in the renewal and had ministries which fostered charismatic renewal among Orthodox Christians.

For the most part, Pentecostalism was scorned by the mainline Protestant churches. Over time it was welcomed by Episcopal or Anglican bishops as a way to bring life to their parishes. A report by a commission of American Episco-

pal bishops in 1962 accepted the renewal into the church provided that the participants continue to participate in the life of the church. This example was followed by other Anglican churches, and the neo-Pentecostal movement came to incorporate many clergy and bishops, as well as thousands of lay members, throughout the world. Similar movements took place in the Lutheran, Presbyterian, and other Protestant churches.

The undoubted pioneer in the effort of reaching out to other churches was the South African-born pastor **David du Plessis.** When du Plessis relocated to the United States in 1948, he began to develop ecumenical ties, first with the National and World Councils of Churches, and then with the Catholic Church. He attended the Second Vatican Council as the accredited Pentecostal observer, although not officially representing any Pentecostal church.

> 66
> *My friends, I said, if you will take the great truths of the Gospel out of your theological deep freezers and get them on the fire of the Holy Spirit, your churches will yet turn the world upside down.*
> 99 *David du Plessis*

Catholic Charismatic Renewal

The Charismatic Renewal in the Catholic Church began in 1967, but the ground had been prepared for by a group of young Catholics who were looking for a revival of faith in the Church in the years during and immediately following the Second Vatican Council.

This group, which began to coalesce at the University of Notre Dame in South Bend, Indiana, in late 1963, included Bert Ghezzi, a graduate student in history, George Martin, a graduate student in philosophy, and Steve Clark, another philosophy graduate student.

Clark, who emerged as the leader of the group, had converted to Christianity during his undergraduate days at Yale University, where he had noticed that those Catholics who associated with other Christians were usually more likely to grow in faith and holiness.

Since he had a convert's zeal to share his faith, he was distressed that many of his fellow Catholic students seemed indifferent:

"They tended to feel that everyone was basically a Christian and that all that was needed was an improvement in society's moral tone."

He graduated from Yale in 1962 and spent the following year studying in Tübingen, Germany, before entering graduate school at Notre Dame. In the summers of 1961 and 1962, Clark went on mission to Mexico. Before setting out, he learned about the Cursillo movement, and while in Mexico, he had the opportunity to meet participants in it.

Through his experiences at Yale and in Mexico, Clark had developed a vision of the church as a community. In 1963, while he was still in Germany, he wrote: →

> Christ wants the man, and he wants the man in a personal relationship—love.
>
> That is why the center of any Christian endeavor must be the community of people who are united to Christ and each other.
>
> They have a common vision, and they have a common spirit because the gift of Christ is the Holy Spirit who moves them to activity.
>
> The church is a community that works together, not simply a service station where individuals and families come together periodically to be fueled up with grace so they can go out and do their jobs.
>
> It is a personal relationship between Christ and his people, not an organizational structure.

Clark saw in Cursillo a way both to encourage the personal relationship with Christ that would be necessary for this vision and to build the community that would result from the shared call to this relationship.

Soon after his arrival at Notre Dame, Clark arranged for a Cursillo to be given. It was attended by George Martin, Bert Ghezzi, and several other active Catholic graduate students and professors.

The second Cursillo at Notre Dame, held in early 1964, witnessed the conversion of Ralph Martin. An undergraduate studying philosophy with a special interest in Nietzsche, he had thrown off his Catholic upbringing and become an outspoken atheist.

Several other students and faculty members also made Cursillos and joined the group.

These included Kevin Ranaghan, a theology student, and his wife Dorothy; Fr. Charles Harris, one of the priests on the faculty; Dr. Paul DeCelles, a physics professor; and undergraduates Jim Cavnar and Gerry Rauch. All of these would later play a role in the emergence of charismatic renewal and the formation of covenant community. Ralph Martin graduated in 1964 and went to Princeton for graduate study, but he rejoined Steve Clark the following year for an extended retreat at Mount Savior, a Benedictine monastery near Elmira, New York. There they felt a call to devote themselves to full-time Christian work.

They abandoned their graduate studies and eventually went to East Lansing, Michigan, where they worked for the National Secretariat of the Cursillo Movement and on the staff of St. John's, the Catholic student parish for Michigan State University.

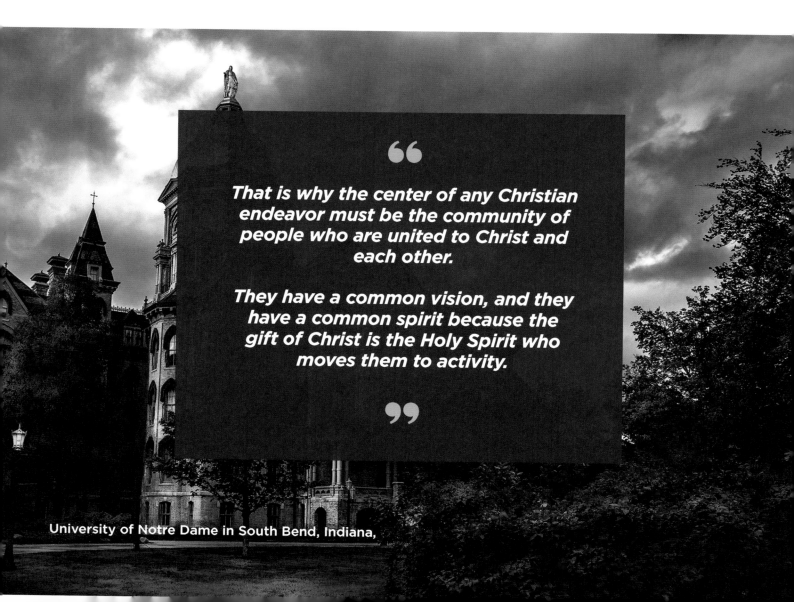

"

That is why the center of any Christian endeavor must be the community of people who are united to Christ and each other.

They have a common vision, and they have a common spirit because the gift of Christ is the Holy Spirit who moves them to activity.

"

University of Notre Dame in South Bend, Indiana,

The Duquesne Weekend

In a nearby state, William Storey William Storey and Ralph Kiefer, two professors at Duquesne University in Pittsburgh, Pennsylvania, planned a student retreat for 17-19 February 1967 and asked the students to prepare for it by reading the Book of Acts and *The Cross and the Switchblade*.

They also invited an Episcopalian woman, who had introduced them to a Pentecostal prayer meeting, to be one of the speakers.

They did not tell the students about Pentecostalism, nor did they pray with them to be baptized in the Holy Spirit. They left that up to God. What followed is known in charismatic circles as **"The Duquesne Weekend."**

On Saturday of the retreat, the first talk dealt with the first two chapters of Acts, while the second talk, only fifteen minutes long, was given by the Episcopalian woman.
Speaking about the gifts of the Spirit, she told the students, **"This still happens today."**

This stirred some of the students to further interest and led that evening to a remarkable outpouring of the Spirit on some of the students gathered. By the end of the retreat, about half of the approximately thirty participants had been baptized in the Holy Spirit.

Testimony 💬

"The Duquesne Weekend is generally accepted as the beginning of the Charismatic Renewal in the Catholic Church. This was the first event at which a group of Catholics experienced the Baptism in the Spirit and the charismatic gifts.
*Through letters, phone calls, and personal visits, word was spreading like wildfire about the pentecostal experience. One of the professors who was a leader on the Duquesne Weekend reported to his friends at Notre Dame, "I don't have to believe in Pentecost, because **I've seen it."***

Patti Mansfield Gallagher, taken from *As by a New Pentecost* ©1992

The early prayer meetings

The charismatic experience began to spread through the Cursillo network. On 5 March 1967, Kiefer came to South Bend and prayed with a group, including the Ranaghans, at Bert Ghezzi's apartment.

Martin and Clark traveled to Pittsburgh to receive prayer. Charismatic prayer groups sprung up in Notre Dame and East Lansing.

In one of the early prayer meetings, the small group heard a prophetic message telling them:

"You will reap a harvest you did not sow...I will send many to you... A shining white cross of my body, of those you work with, will be raised up among you."

The fifteen or so participants who heard that word had no idea of the fruit that would grow from this little meeting.

Organizing Community

In order to be more than an informal environment, a basic Christian community requires organization.

Much of the organizational model of our covenant communities derived from the Cursillo movement.

In December 1968, Steve Clark wrote a *"state of the union"* message for Fr. Harris and some of the other leaders, discussing the progress of the mission and the prospects for its future.

He made some proposals for the development of the new student movement:

1. Organize the fourteen leaders of the group into teams, each with a particular concern. Fr. Harris should take overall responsibility as "overall caaoordinator," or that the position should rotate: until then, Clark had been the de facto leader.

2. There could be a meeting on Monday nights "other than Thursday, to which we only invite students who have received the baptism, which would be a chance to grow in the life of the Spirit…. **It could be a focus for the creation of a sense of community among the regulars, too."**

3. There could be **small "growth groups"** similar to Cursillo group reunions, to facilitate growth in the Christian life among the students, and smaller prayer meetings for study in university dormitories and other situations.

4. More people should be added to the leadership group, and there could be special groups to train students who appeared to have gifts for pastoral work.

The Word of God

The first community to adopt a covenant

In order to trace the beginnings of covenant community, we will focus on how the first community to adopt a covenant, the Word of God community in Ann Arbor, Michigan (USA), experienced God leading them to make a covenant with him and with one another.

Commitment and Membership

The earliest element of organization in the Ann Arbor community was the adoption of a definite commitment to the community that developed from simple participation in the Monday prayer meetings. Membership in the community was defined by that commitment.

At their 1970 conference, the community adopted a name, The Word of God, as well as a structure. The commitment to the community became a public declaration:

"I want to give my life fully to God and live as a member of The Word of God."

After the first two groups had made the public commitment, the community introduced the "underway" status for those who were approaching full membership.

The public commitment and the underway commitment have remained features of many communities, including those in the Sword of the Spirit.

Leadership

The Word of God's leadership grew from the original four men (Steve Clark, Ralph Martin, Jim Cavnar, and Gerry Rauch) into a larger council that guided community activities. The leaders who governed the community were called **coordinators**.

This name suggested that their function was to "coordinate" or organize the work of other leaders, but the description of their work went beyond that. They were also charged, as a group, with overall responsibility for the life of the community and with training others to be leaders.

Other leadership and service roles for both men and women emerged in the community over time to 'build up the body and equip the saints for ministry'.

 The public commitment and the underway commitment have remained features of many communities, including those in the Sword of the Spirit.

The Naming of the Community

The larger the community grew, the more pressing became the need to have a name by which others could call them. The more the Lord made them into a people together, the more it made sense to have a name of their own.

During a meeting in which they considered the name, the two most compelling proposals seemed to be "Community of the Savior" and "Community of the Resurrection". At the last moment, another name, "Community of The Word of God" was added because of a passage that had been prayed for about the name. The passage came from the Book of Revelation:

> " Then I saw heaven opened, and behold, a white horse! He who sat upon it is called Faithful and True, and in righteousness he judges and makes war. His eyes are like a flame of fire, and on his head are many diadems, and he has a name inscribed which no one knows but himself. He is clad in a robe dipped in blood, and the name by which he is called is The Word of God. And the armies of heaven, arrayed in fine linen, white and pure, followed him on white horses. From his mouth issues a sharp sword with which to smite the nations, and he will rule them with a rod of iron; he will tread the winepress of the fury of the wrath of God the Almighty. On his robe and on his thigh, he has a name inscribed, King of kings and Lord of lords. *Rev 19:11-16* "

Then, right at the end of the meeting, two prophecies were given. The message of the first was,

"You are my people. I formed you — you are mine, therefore you shall be called by my own name."

In the second prophecy, the Lord spoke and said that they were taking the question of the name too lightly. The name was important. They needed to seek the Lord to find the name because he wanted to give them a name himself.

In response, the members of the community then set aside a special day of prayer and fasting, and gathered together to seek the Lord—not so much to ask for the name but to present themselves to him, and to give room for God to speak to them and show them how they should present themselves before him. At that gathering, He spoke about his love for them and how they needed to be purified. Finally, he spoke to them through this prophecy:

Turn Page ⤶

Listen to me: listen carefully to me, so that you can believe the promises that I make to you.

The promises which I make to you are far beyond your comprehension— listen to me so that you can believe them. My promises are certain.

I, and those who are with me, call you **'The Word of God'** because you are my word now to the whole face of the earth. I have called you and I have created you, not for your own sake, but for my sake and for the sake of all of those whom I would gather to myself.

I am going to give you my Spirit in a way in which I have never given my Spirit to any people. I am going to make you my people in a way in which I have never before made any people my people. I am going to pour out upon you a spirit of power and of grandeur and of glory so that all who see you will know that I am God and that I am among you.

Therefore, this is my word to you.

You have been first in all of my thoughts; have I been first in all of your thoughts? I have in every way come to you; have you in every way come to me? I have poured myself out to you, and given myself to you, without reserve; have you given yourselves entirely to me?

Seek me. I have already sought you. Look to me. Make me first in your lives. I have become your God, and I have made you my people. Look to me. Seek me.

First Commitment to the Covenant

When the community went on retreat in the early autumn of 1970, the leaders presented several proposals: the new name The Word of God; an explicit public commitment to the covenant; division into defined subcommunities; and a leadership structure.

The community accepted the proposals, **and on 28 September 1970, the first ninety-nine people made a public commitment to the covenant of The Word of God**, followed by another group of fifty-four on 23 November.

The original Foundations in Christian Living course, which was taught to people entering the community following their participation in the Life in the Spirit Seminars, now had a sequel, Foundations in Christian Living II, which covered more teaching on living in community. It was divided into separate tracks for single men, single women, and married couples.

Before new participants made an underway commitment or began the Foundations courses, they attended a Community Weekend in which they learned about the call to Christian community.

The Introduction of the Covenant

What did *"covenant"* mean in the context of a Christian community?

The need for community was something already intended from the Cursillo days at Notre Dame. But when the Ann Arbor community began receiving prophetic words during 1970 speaking of a covenant, they were puzzled. Many of the leaders were trained in theology and Scripture and were familiar with the word, *"covenant."* God had made a covenant with Israel and Christ was the high priest of the New Covenant. But what did it mean to say that God wanted to make a covenant with them as a people?

As they studied the scriptural references, a new dimension of their call to community emerged. This perspective was crucial to their identity, not merely as a community, but as a covenant community.

- The call to covenant is at God's initiative.

The whole idea of *"covenant"* came prophetically from God—it was his initiative. Community was already forming, but *"covenant"* added something crucial to the kind of community the Lord was calling them to become.

- This call is also a call to mission.

The covenant was a call to members to dedicate themselves to the service of God, not merely as individuals, but as members of a body, taking their places within the whole Christian people.

The nature of this mission involved calling men and women to Christ and sharing with them the life in the Holy Spirit.

- The covenant with God also involves a covenant relationship among the members.

They were to love one another with a love founded in a common calling.

They were brothers and sisters in Christ, a relationship they shared with all other Christians, but by entering into the community covenant they were brothers and sisters bound to one another in a special way, in a bond created by God as his own initiative.

The mutual commitment that was the heart of our covenant together came before the details of a way of life or a specific mission.

> "And I will establish my covenant between me and you and your offspring after you throughout their generations for an everlasting covenant, to be God to you and to your offspring after you. And I will give to you and to your offspring after you the land of your sojournings, all the land of Canaan, for an everlasting possession, and I will be their God."

Genesis 17:7-9

People from the community in East Lansing MI, USA.

The Community of Communities

Ann Arbor was by no means the only place where community developed. The process occurred in parallel ways in other places in the U.S, including South Bend, where many members of the original Notre Dame Cursillo group remained, and in East Lansing, Michigan, where one of the earliest charismatic prayer groups had arisen.

Development in these communities paralleled that of The Word of God in Ann Arbor: the establishment of a stable leadership group, the adoption of a name, and the explicit commitment to a covenant.

As the communities themselves adopted more formal structures, the communities began to develop more formal ties with one another.

Leaders in these communities were in touch with the leaders of The Word of God, and they gave and received mutual help and encouragement.

Community building became international in 1975, on the occasion of the International Catholic Charismatic Renewal conference held in Rome.

Immediately after the conference, Cardinal Suenens, Archbishop of Malines-Brussels, leader of the Catholic Church in Belgium and a man of significant influence at the Second Vatican Council, invited Ralph Martin and Steve Clark to move to Brussels. Ralph Martin and his family (along with several single men and women in his household), Steve Clark with a household of the Servants of the Word, and another family moved to Brussels in August 1976. In addition to working with Cardinal Suenens in developing the international charismatic renewal, they began forming a community.

Members of the People of Praise, as well as members of the People of Hope in New Jersey and the Alleluia Community in Augusta, Georgia, joined those from The Word of God in building up this work.

In late 1975, shortly before the outreach work in Belgium began, seventeen members of a growing community in Beirut, Lebanon, moved to The Word of God.

The group in Beirut had begun when Peter Shebaya, in 1969, encountered the charismatic renewal in Ann Arbor through his friend Paul Melton, a member of The Word of God.

Although civil war had erupted in Lebanon, their goal in coming to Ann Arbor was not to escape the war but to learn about community. They remained for seven months and returned home after Easter of 1976 with war still raging, convinced that the Lord had called them to form a community in Beirut in spite of the difficulties. They became the People of God community, and are still flourishing in Lebanon with outreaches throughout the Middle East.

In 1978, local leaders from London were sent to a conference in Belgium, held under the auspices of Cardinal Suenens. They were baptized in the Holy Spirit and returned to London convinced that there should be a covenant community in London. An invitation was extended by the Catholic Archbishop of Westminster and the Anglican Bishop of Kensington, to build an ecumenical charismatic community in London.

In September of 1979, several members of The Word of God, the People of Praise, and the People of Hope, some of whom had previously served in Belgium, moved to London.

This group included members of the Servants of the Word, who set up the household that still exists there. Several long-time leaders in the charismatic renewal in the London area joined them and formed what is now the Antioch Community.

A small ecumenical group of students in Costa Rica decided to open a café to outreach to other students. They ran evangelistic camps twice a year.

During one of these camps, they experienced a "Pentecost" and received the first call to community life. After a few years, the Agape Community was formed which later changed its name to Arbol de Vida.

In 1975 the Lord began speaking to Carlos Mántica, a Cursillo leader in Nicaragua, about building a wall. Of course, he had no idea what that meant. Some time later, not only did he know certainly that the Lord wanted to start a covenant community in Managua, but he even knew what it should be called. It would be called The City of God! By the end of 1977, he and a few other leaders made a covenant commitment ant the community started.

"It all started with an experience that God is real, not a distant God. His love is personal". This was the experience of a handful of men and women who frequented a weekly prayer meeting in Makati City, Philippines. In 1975, 41 men and women gathered together for a retreat and the Lord spoke to them. This is the beginning of Ligaya ng Panginoon.

The Prophecy of the Bulwark

"

With their shared outreach expanding, The Word of God and the People of Praise drew closer together as communities. In July 1975, the two communities held a joint retreat at Adrian College in Adrian, Michigan. During this conference, **they received what has become a very important prophetic word for the Sword of the Spirit.**

Listen to me now, listen to me today, while I reveal to you a part of my mind, while I speak to you of things to come. I have brought you together here to be the beginning of something very important in my church. I have brought you together here to join you together and to give you a vision of what is to come.

I am raising up other communities all around this world, and I will want them to join together with you and to be together with you in unity.

And I will raise up individuals around this world and I will rally them to you and bind them fast to you and make you one. Yes, I will to do that as a source of strength for my church.

I will make you a bulwark to defend against the onslaught of the enemy those who are not prepared, those who are not ready. I will not have them swept away because they are not ready, but I will protect them behind the bulwark that I form out of you. I want you to be ready to join yourselves with others and to stand together with them in battle against the onslaught that is coming and to defend the weak, and to defend those who are confused, and to protect those who are not prepared until I am able to fulfill my entire plan.

I tell you, you are a part and you are not the whole. You are a part and you are not the whole.

There are many other things that I am doing in this world today, there are many other ways that I am at work to raise up my people in strength and in glory. You are a part and not the whole. I want you to take your part seriously and to lay your lives down for it, but I want you to understand that only I see the entire plan, only I see every front of this battle. I will raise you up together with others and bind you together to make you a bulwark, but that is not all there is to be, because when you have stemmed the onslaught of the enemy then I will reveal to you greater things. In the unity you have with one another, there is a foreshadowing and a prefigurement of something much greater, much more vast, much more glorious I will unveil at that time. You are a foreshadowing and a prefigurement; you are a bulwark that I have set up to stem the onslaught of the enemy; you are a part and not the whole; you are my servants and my people. **Lay down your lives now for the things that I have revealed to you. Commit yourselves to them so that in the day of battle you can stand fast and prove victorious with me.**

"

Relations among communities

1977

The Association of Communities

The Association of Communities: The Word of God and the People of Praise sought a way to formalize their relationship. In the late 1977, after a consultation among all the members, the two communities agreed to an underway covenant relationship. They made formal visitations to one another, and they hosted training institutes and meetings to help form their leaders.

1980

The Association breaks down and The Federation of Communities is formed.

After several years of working together, it became clear that the leaders of the People of Praise and those of The Word of God had different approaches to developing the life of the community and the Association was unable to proceed. Some communities left. The rest of the Association, including those in the United States, Europe, Latin America, and Asia, renamed their group the Federation of Communities and continued to seek closer ties and shared outreach.

1982

The Sword of the Spirit: a new ecumenical community of communities

In June 1982, the leaders of The Word of God decided to establish a new grouping of communities called the Sword of the Spirit. This was to take the form of an international, ecumenical community of locally governed communities, but united under a single, international government. All the communities in the Federation along with some other communities who had a relationship with the Word of God were invited to join the Sword of the Spirit.

2020

The Sword of the Spirit is a growing "community of communities"

With more than 93 communities (both full member communities and those investigating our life) from around the world.

Our call to be Ecumenical

From the very beginning of covenant community life, many of the leaders and members shared a deep conviction that living as an ecumenical community was a foundational element of their call. The earliest covenant communities were ecumenical in membership and remain so. This often involves Catholics and Protestants living together but, in several communities, also includes members from Eastern and Oriental Orthodox churches. We rejoice that Orthodox, Protestants, and Catholics can share a common covenant way of life together in Christ.

Each local community in the Sword of the Spirit, whether ecumenical or Catholic or Orthodox in membership, shares and supports our common ecumenical calling. The Sword of the Spirit today remains an international, ecumenical community of communities, living out a call from God to demonstrate that Christians from diverse traditions can live and serve together in unity.

We have adopted the term **"ecumenical"** instead of alternative terms such as *"nondenominational"* or *"interdenominational."* The term *"ecumenical"* indicates, first, that members of the community do not give up their connection to a Christian church body. In fact, we encourage and expect our members to be active participants in their churches.

Secondly, the term *"ecumenical"* indicates that the members of the community enter into the covenant relationship as individual Christians, recognizing their fellow members as brothers and sisters in Christ, rather than as representatives of a church or Christian tradition. As an international community, we anchor our teaching on the Scriptures and the Nicene Creed and seek to express our teaching in a way acceptable to Christians of all traditions.

In 2008 a new grouping, the Association of Ecumenical Communities (AEC), with its own Council, was formed to include the ecumenical communities. Its purpose was to ensure that concerns for the ecumenical nature of the Sword of the Spirit and the needs of ecumenical communities would be met. In 2016, this was changed to become the Ecumenical Commission which is representative of all the communities in the Sword of the Spirit and promotes ecumenical life throughout the Sword of the Spirit.

Coordinators' embrace of respect and peace

Supporting one another in daily life

Households

In the beginning, the most basic unit of The Word of God was the household.

Households originally were groups of single people living together in one house or apartment. They were also the smallest pastoral unit of the community, with one member being pastorally responsible for the other members.

"Households" in dormitories formed as groupings of people living in student housing came together to share a common life. Other "non-residential households" provided a way for small groups for individuals or couples to come together in a shared life.

As the community grew, households that consisted of a married couple and their children along with several single men and women became more common.

Men's household in Beirut

Women's household in Ann Arbor

Cell Groups

In early 1977, the community in Ann Arbor began to move from the household as the basic unit to men's and women's groups, generally ranging in size from four to nine people.

Most of these comprised people of the same state in life and roughly the same age.

As the large households that had characterized the early 1970s began to dissolve—often because the growing families had less room for unrelated singles—men's and women's groups seemed to meet the needs of the new situation more effectively.

Since this time, these small groups have been the basic unit for supporting one another in daily life for communities in the Sword of the Spirit.

A Difficult Decade

The 1980s were difficult years for the Sword of the Spirit, and most particularly for communities in the United States. These difficulties were due to a number of factors:

- The first attempts to bring the communities together were not fully successful, causing relationship strains and questions about organization.
- Fears about "cult" groups in the wider culture put pressure on several of our communities and made attempts at organization more difficult.
- Major pastoral issues within the Word of God community caused some people to question the model and to consider other approaches.

In 1989-1990, the head coordinators of the Word of God community initiated a process of leaving the Sword of the Spirit (remaining in an "allied" relationship). Several other communities joined them.

In Ann Arbor, some of the coordinators and a significant minority of members decided to remain in the Sword of the Spirit, leading to the formation of a new Sword of the Spirit community (now called Word of Life).

These difficulties led to a season of re-examination of the fundamental elements of covenant life together. It was a season of humility and brokenness, a season to reflect and consider and listen to the Lord.

In order to respond constructively to these challenges, the Council of the Sword of the Spirit began a thorough examination of all the elements of common life, continuing for several years and including the methods of giving pastoral care.

Reform and Moving Forward

In 1990, the second Sword of the Spirit Assembly agreed on a new constitution, making the Sword of the Spirit a "community of communities" organized around a federal structure rather than under one common government. This approach was decided on as the best way to balance unity and diversity in our international life.

In that year, Carlos Mántica, from the community in Managua, Nicaragua, became president of the Council of the Sword of the Spirit. Since then there have been four other presidents: Carlos Alonso Vargas from the Arbol de Vida Community in San José, Costa Rica (1993-1998), David McGill from The Community of the Risen Christ in Scotland (1998-2003), Steve Clark from the Servants of the Word (2003-2009), and Jean Barbara from the People of God community in Beirut (2009-present).

The International Assembly is the highest leadership body of the Sword of the Spirit. It meets every two years. It is responsible to review and approve the policies and the teachings that are followed by all the member communities. It is also a forum for the leaders to provide and receive personal support, relationship-building, communication of vision, and sharing of experience that strengthen the life and mission of the Sword of the Spirit.

The International Executive Council, led by the President of the Sword of the Spirit, is the leadership team that maintains and moves forward our common life and work. It is an executive body that directs the work we do on the international level.

The International Women's Coordinating Council take an overall concern for the life and care of women in the Sword of the Spirit. They are supported in this task by women's leadership councils in each of our regions.

Most local communities are grouped into four established 'regions' (Asia, Europe & the Middle East, Ibero-America, and North America). The Sword of the Spirit also has communities in the South Pacific. Each region is led by a regional council. These regions are the primary places for strengthening the communities, building relationships and unity, caring for local communities and community support programs, hosting regional youth programs, and providing leaders' formation programs.

Some regions are also further divided into geographic or culturally-specific 'zones' to further develop and support our life.

Patterns of Prayer

Starting with the Servants of the Word, The Word of God community began to develop shared patterns of prayer, and these were adopted by many families and individuals in the community.

The most important of these was the ceremony for setting apart Sunday as **the Lord's Day,** developed in the late 1970s by the Servants of the Word and spread to other households.

In November 1980, The Word of God coordinators published the Lord's Day ceremony, along with a set of daily family prayers, and asked members of the community to use these in their homes. Along with the prayers for opening the Lord's Day, teachings were developed about the significance of keeping the Lord's Day holy, free from "weekday thoughts and cares."

The coordinators also began to encourage the observance of the seasons of Advent as a preparation for Christmas, and the Forty Days (of Lent) leading up to the feast of Easter. Community gatherings during these times adopted special themes to observe these Christian seasons.

This concern for the weekly and annual rhythms of life, and particularly the setting aside of the Lord's Day, remains an important feature of life in the Sword of the Spirit.

As an evangelical, I have discovered the relevance of the liturgical seasons in our Christian practice. Even though I still have questions about the Catholic liturgical calendar, I thank God for being able to enjoy these seasons along with my brothers and sisters.

Rebecca Calvo
Arbol de Vida Community

Living Single for the Lord

The Servants of the Word

In the early 1970s, the development of a celibate brotherhood of single men within the Ann Arbor community was a turning point in community life and outreach.

When Steve Clark, Ralph Martin, Jim Cavnar, and Gerry Rauch came to Ann Arbor in 1967, they were all single men and saw themselves as, at least for a time, fully dedicated to Christian service. The rest of the team who joined them in 1968 consciously took the same approach, not least because, as full-time apostolic workers, they had to live very simply for financial reasons.

Ralph Martin married in 1968, Jim Cavnar in 1969, and Gerry Rauch in 1972. However, several men who became leaders in the community (including six of the original eleven coordinators) felt called to a life of celibacy—to "living single for the Lord," to use their preferred term. Most of them lived in a household with Steve Clark, first at 500 Packard Street in Ann Arbor and later at 335 Packard Street, where they would meet to study various historical rules for celibate community life such as those of St. Francis of Assisi, St. Basil the Great, and St. Benedict.

At Pentecost in 1971, Steve Clark and seven other men made a temporary commitment to live "single for the Lord" for one year. Later that year they developed a statement of their commitment and way of life, their "covenant," and began to live together as a brotherhood.

In January 1974, Steve Clark and four other men made lifelong commitments to live single for the Lord in the brotherhood, a commitment repeated in a public ceremony in February.

The first brothers were Catholics but had always intended to be open to Protestant and Orthodox brothers. The first Protestant brothers began to make commitments in late 1975.

More brothers joined; later that year, there were two households of men. In January 1976, they received a name: the Servants of the Word.

The Servants of the Word have since grown into a worldwide brotherhood, with houses in the United States, the United Kingdom, Mexico, Costa Rica, the Philippines, and Lebanon. They have often been in the forefront of spearheading new outreach ventures in the Sword of the Spirit.

Other Expressions

A sisterhood of women living single for the Lord, The Servants of God's Love, also formed within the Word of God community in the 1970s. They are now flourishing as a distinct Catholic religious community. Several of these original sisters came together with other single women from around the world to form Bethany Association, an international, ecumenical association of women living single for the Lord in the Sword of the Spirit.

The Brotherhood of Hope is a Catholic religious community of men within the Sword of the Spirit, with several households in the USA (Florida, Massachusetts, New Jersey, and Minnesota).

Pronto 2020 was a worldwide online event that gathered more than 2000 young professionals from around the Sword of the Spirit.

PART 2

Ongoing Mission and Outreach

The Sword of the Spirit Today is a worldwide network of communities, pursuing mission in many places and many forms. Providing a comprehensive picture of the outreach efforts of the Sword of the Spirit on the local, regional, and international levels would require a great deal more space than is available here.

Accordingly, we have chosen to describe some of the early history of mission efforts, and then have highlighted a few outreaches from the large number that are active today.

Service to the Catholic Charismatic Renewal

The Pentecostal movement, and later the Charismatic Renewal, began with people who were eager to bring others to Christ. Therefore, it is not surprising that the impetus for mission was at the heart of the Renewal and of the covenant communities that arose within the Renewal.

Much of this mission was informal: one friend brought another to a prayer meeting, where he or she encountered the power of the Holy Spirit.

As the Renewal grew, however, the impulse to mission began to take the form of organized outreach and service. Initially, this was expressed through internal organizations to foster the Renewal itself, resulting in hundreds of thousands of people coming to a deeper relationship with the Lord and receiving the power of the Holy Spirit.

1967

First International Conference on the Charismatic Renewal, South Bend.

1969

1975

An international (general) conference in 1975 is held in Rome, bringing people from all over the world, and culminating in an audience with Pope Paul VI in which he gives his encouragement to the Charismatic Renewal movement.

1973

The Committee decides to begin an International Communications Office (ICO).

1976

The ICO moves to Brussels, Belgium. It later moves to Rome and changes its name to International Catholic Charismatic Renewal Services (ICCRS).

Outreach members move to Belgium

Steve Clark suggests "that we stop using the term 'Pentecostal Movement' and instead use the term 'Charismatic Renewal'. This approach is adopted.

1969

Annual Conferences for training of leaders begin

1970

The leaders of the Renewal decide to set up a committee to oversee the services provided by the Ann Arbor and South Bend communities—the Catholic Charismatic Renewal Service Committee (CCRSC)

The CCRSC, incorporated as Charismatic Renewal Services (CRS), oversees the work of the Communication Center responsible for the annual international conferences and the Pastoral Newsletter put out by the Ann Arbor community called "New Covenant."

1971

CHARIS

2017

An anniversary celebrating 50 years of the Catholic Charismatic Renewal is held in Rome.

2019

A new, Vatican international vehicle for Catholic Charismatic Renewal, called "Charis," is founded, as a part of the new Dicastery for Laity and Family.

Ecumenical Outreach

Because of the strong conviction that covenant communities were called to work ecumenically, early leaders worked with pastors and teachers from a variety of church backgrounds.

The greatest achievement of this cooperative effort was the 1977 Conference for the Charismatic Renewal in the Christian Churches in Kansas City that drew together 50,000 people in Arrowhead Stadium.

In 1977, leaders of the Work of Christ Community in Lansing, Michigan, U.S.A. teamed up with two Orthodox priests to form the Service Committee for Orthodox Charismatic Renewal which began to organize annual Orthodox Charismatic conferences.

In October 1980, a meeting of Catholic and Evangelical Protestant pastors, scholars, and writers was held in Ann Arbor who devoted themselves to consider the place of Christianity in the midst of the modern world and its challenges.

Papers from this meeting were published the following year as Christianity Confronts Modernity, and similar conferences were held throughout the 1980s.

Publishing

Publishing began on a modest scale. In the late 1960s, in order to maintain communication with the emerging but far-flung movement, the leaders in Ann Arbor began sending out a mimeographed newsletter edited by Ralph Martin.

Originally entitled the "Pastoral Newsletter," by 1970 the publication developed from a few stapled sheets to a small magazine. In July 1971, this became "New Covenant" magazine, subtitled "The Monthly Magazine of the Catholic Charismatic Renewal."

Soon the community in Ann Arbor began publishing books through another "basement" outreach, Word of Life publishing. The first book published was Fr. George Montague's *Riding the Wind*.

Word of Life expanded, publishing, for example, the team manual for the Life in the Spirit Seminars (1973). In 1976, Word of Life became Servant Publications.

In the 1980s, Servant Books began reaching a wider audience, publishing books by leading Evangelicals: J. I. Packer, Donald Bloesch, Harry Blamires, and Elizabeth Eliot.

Many of Servant's books are still in print with other publishing houses, including Franciscan Publications and Ignatius Press.

In 1978 The Service Committee for Orthodox Charismatic Renewal began publishing Theosis, a monthly periodical serving the Orthodox Charismatic Renewal.

Members and leaders of the Work of Christ Community served Theosis in editorial, publishing, and distribution roles.

> ℹ️ **"The not-for-profit company had annual sales of about $4 million and published about 50 titles per year."**

Music
and Worship

Music has always been a feature of charismatic prayer meetings. At the time the charismatic renewal began, the songs featured at prayer meetings were drawn from older Protestant Pentecostal and Evangelical music, new worship music current in Catholic circles, and a few traditional hymns (e.g. "Holy God, We Praise Thy Name").

Prayer groups and communities proved to be fertile sources of new worship songs.

In particular, The Word of God in Ann Arbor produced many new songs.

In an effort to acquaint the wider renewal movement with the new music, The Word of God music ministry issued its first record in 1972 entitled "Songs of The Word of God."

In the years that followed, The Word of God Music, which became part of Servant Publications, issued several further albums. In 1975, Servant published a song book "*Songs of Praise*," followed by three supplemental volumes, which finally were published in a combined edition.

Sword of the Spirit communities continue to be a source of new worship songs.

Many authors, including a younger generation, have written songs which have spread across our network of communities and are used in prayer meetings in many countries and in many languages.

As one example, the Music Ministry from Jésed community in Monterrey, México has become a widely known group in all of Latin America.

With more than 60 music albums, they regularly perform evangelistic concerts and help lead the music at wider prayer events. In 2017, Jésed served during the Pope's visit to Mexico.

Mission around the World

Many communities around the world also developed local outreaches of various kinds.

For many years, the People of Hope in New Jersey ran "Jesus Weeks," evangelistic rallies that drew many thousands, as well as taking responsibility for organizing regional conferences for the charismatic renewal.

In Monterrey, Mexico, Jésed community has, among other outreaches, established a mission to married couples which now numbers over 1500 married couples.

The example of Ligaya ng Panginoon

Ligaya ng Panginoon ("Joy of the Lord") in Manila, Philippines, is at present the largest community in the Sword of the Spirit, and also has the most extensive outreaches.

"Ligaya was like an atom, so small and yet so full of energy that it was almost ready to explode into action. Some members wanted to go out and bring Ligaya to serve the poor. Others wanted to do healing sessions. We had social activists too. Still, others just wanted to serve where there were invitations to serve from other prayer groups."

Vic Gutierrez

1975

Ligaya's first outreach, begun in 1975, was Word of Joy Foundation, a publishing house that reprinted and distributed literature on the charismatic renewal, including New Covenant magazine, in the Philippines and elsewhere in Asia.

1980

In 1980, the community began a weekly meeting of business executives that grew into the Brotherhood of Christian Businessmen and Professionals. That same year they also started an outreach to university students that became Christ's Youth in Action (CYA).

1981

Perhaps the most extensive movement that began in Ligaya was Couples for Christ. It began as an outreach in 1981 and spread throughout the Philippines and beyond in the following years.

1993

Familia, a movement to strengthen family life in parishes, began in 1993.

1986

In 1986, Ligaya began to form small communities among the poor of Manila called Tahanan ng Panginoon (House of the Lord).

1984

Ang Lingkod ng Panginoon (The Servant of the Lord), an outreach to single professionals, began in 1984.

1998

In 1998, Ligaya founded a school, now called Cradle of Joy Catholic Progressive School.

Members of Ligaya also founded Pathways, an evangelistic movement that operates in ten sites, and airs a radio program called **"Kakaiba Ka!" – "You Are Different!**

One of Ligaya's most important activities has been helping to found other communities, many of which are now members of the Sword of the Spirit. Groups from Ligaya have helped develop communities in other parts of the Philippines, in India and Singapore, and have carried out evangelistic missions in Indonesia, Thailand, China, and other parts of Asia. Ligaya's community-building outreach has gone beyond Asia thanks to the Filipino diaspora, mainly in North America.

Building Communities

Thanks to the steadfastness and vision of many leaders and the perseverance in daily life by normal members in our communities, this "community of communities" was able to weather the difficulties of the 1980s and early 1990s and move forward in common life and mission.

While the communities in the Sword the Spirit have many different outreaches, the principal mission of the Sword of the Spirit as a whole is **building new communities** to strengthen the bulwark of communities around the world that serve to help one another and be a source of help and, at times, a refuge for Christians.

The "Macroschema" for community building, developed in the Ibero-American Region, has become the guide for the development of a community through various stages, culminating in full membership in the Sword of the Spirit.

Communities per Region

8
3
1 1 1
1977-1980

6
3
2
1 1
1980-1982

11
8
6
5
1
1982-1991

37
21
14
15
3
1991-2020

- ■ North American Region
- ■ Europe & Middle East
- ▨ Ibero-american Region
- ▨ Asia
- ■ South Pacific or Other

Throughout the world, new communities are still being formed and joining the network.

Latin America has seen the greatest growth in new communities: as of 2019, there were thirty-seven communities in the Ibero-American Region, which also includes Spain and Portugal and predominantly Spanish-speaking communities in North America.

The Ibero-American region was also the first region to subdivide into "zones" and it currently consists of five zones.

In recent years the Sword of the Spirit has seen new growth in parts of the world where it has not been previously active.

Some communities have joined the Sword of the Spirit after having lived community life for many years. Others are brand new communities. Some have grown like UCO and SPO. A new community in Seattle, Washington, recently began to form when members of other communities in various regions moved to the city for jobs in its growing economy.

In various parts of the world, the Sword of the Spirit has been expanding by establishing university and young professional outreaches and then working with

those evangelized to develop into a community. Over time we have begun to learn about how to plant the seed of community, and how to help it grow and bear fruit.

In 1996, the Lamb of God, an ecumenical community with branches in various cities of New Zealand, affiliated with the Sword of the Spirit. They became a full member community in 2006.

The People of God in Lebanon have fostered and overseen the beginnings of community in Turkey, Syria, Qatar, Israel, and elsewhere. They initiated and have since supported the fledgling community in Aleppo, Syria, in spite of the fierce fighting in that country.

In 2004 a small group of expatriate Filipinos established the community known as God's Light in Sydney, Australia, and in 2015 the Families for Christ community in Melbourne, Australia, became an affiliate community.

We in the Sword of the Spirit have always believed that God called us to intergenerational community.

Leaders of the Lamb of God Community in New Zealand

COMMUNITIES

CANADA
1. Families for Christ Community, Vancouver
2. Jesus the Good Shepherd, Toronto
3. One with God, Toronto
4. Servants of God, Ottawa

UNITED STATES
5. The Brotherhood of Hope, Boston MA
6. El Camino, Westfield MA
7. Community of Christ the Redeemer, St. Paul MN
8. Christ's Ardent Disciples in Action, Detroit MI
9. City on the Hill, Los Angeles CA
10. Familia de Dios, Mission TX
11. Families for Christ, Dallas TX
12. Family of Faith, Newark NJ
13. Fountain of Life, Tallahassee FL
14. Greater Columbus Covenant Community, Columbus OH
15. Light of Christ, Grand Rapids MI
16. The Morning Star Christian Community, Jackson MI
17. Muralla de Dios, Hatillo and Río Piedras, Puerto Rico
18. La Nueva Jerusalén, Miami FL
19. The People of God, Pittsburgh PA
20. The People of Hope, Newark NJ
21. Spirit of Christ, Jacksonville FL
22. The Sword of the Spirit, Seattle WA
23. Triumph of the Cross Community, Frederick MD
24. Word of Life, Ann Arbor MI
25. Work of Christ, East Lansing MI

MEXICO
26. Alianza Eterna, Merida
27. Betania, Acapulco
28. Incienso de Dios, Xalapa
29. Comunidad Jésed, Monterrey
30. Luz Eterna, Querétaro
31. Misericordia de Dios, Zitácuaro
32. Sagrada Familia, Tampico
33. La Sagrada Familia, Veracruz
34. Siloé, San Miguel de Allende
35. Sion, Cuernavaca
36. Verbum Dei, Mexicali

GUATEMALA
37. Comunidad Dios Refugio y Fortaleza, Guatemala City

HONDURAS
38. Comunidad Fortaleza de Dios, San Pedro Sula
39. Oasis del Señor, La Ceiba
40. Victoria de Dios, Tegucigalpa
41. La Viña del Señor, El Mochito

NICARAGUA
42. Ciudad de Dios, Managua
43. Comunidad de Cristo Resucitado, Chontales
44. Pequeña Israel, Granada
45. Templo del Espíritu, Masaya
46. Trono de Dios, Boaco

COSTA RICA
47. Comunidad Árbol de Vida, San José
48. Comunidad Fuente de Vida, Heredia
49. Comunidad Horeb, Guápiles

DOMINICAN REPUBLIC
50. Comunidad Cuerpo de Cristo, Santo Domingo

COLOMBIA
51. Comunidad Emmanuel, Cali
52. El Gozo del Señor, Bogota

ECUADOR
53. Comunidad Jesús es el Señor, Cuenca
54. Comunidad Jesús es el Señor, Quito
55. Tierra Santa, Guayaquil

PERÚ
56. Fuerza de lo Alto, Lima

UNITED KINGDOM
57. The Antioch Community, London, England
58. Charis Community, Belfast, Northern Ireland
59. The Community of the Risen Christ, Glasgow, Scotland

REPUBLIC OF IRELAND
60. Community of Nazareth, Dublin

BELGIUM
61. Jerusalem, Belgium

WORLDWIDE

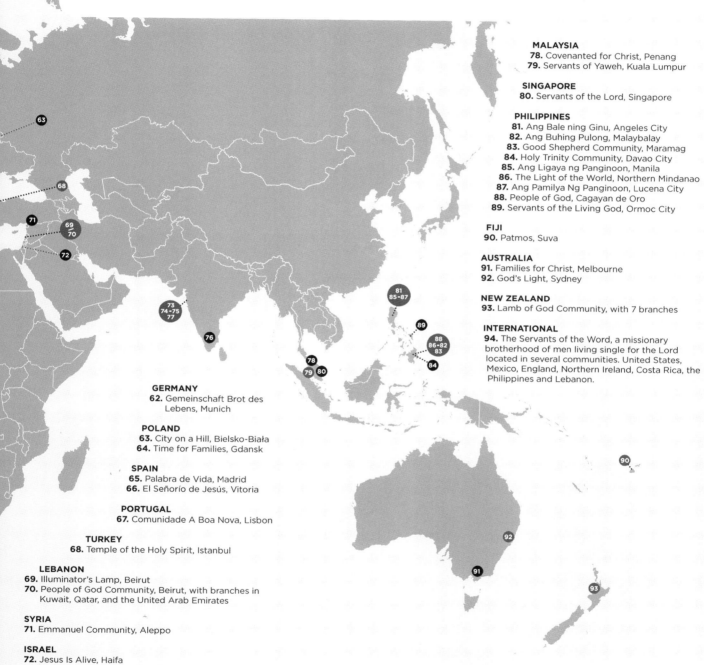

MALAYSIA
78. Covenanted for Christ, Penang
79. Servants of Yaweh, Kuala Lumpur

SINGAPORE
80. Servants of the Lord, Singapore

PHILIPPINES
81. Ang Bale ning Ginu, Angeles City
82. Ang Buhing Pulong, Malaybalay
83. Good Shepherd Community, Maramag
84. Holy Trinity Community, Davao City
85. Ang Ligaya ng Panginoon, Manila
86. The Light of the World, Northern Mindanao
87. Ang Pamilya Ng Panginoon, Lucena City
88. People of God, Cagayan de Oro
89. Servants of the Living God, Ormoc City

FIJI
90. Patmos, Suva

AUSTRALIA
91. Families for Christ, Melbourne
92. God's Light, Sydney

NEW ZEALAND
93. Lamb of God Community, with 7 branches

INTERNATIONAL
94. The Servants of the Word, a missionary brotherhood of men living single for the Lord located in several communities. United States, Mexico, England, Northern Ireland, Costa Rica, the Philippines and Lebanon.

GERMANY
62. Gemeinschaft Brot des Lebens, Munich

POLAND
63. City on a Hill, Bielsko-Biała
64. Time for Families, Gdansk

SPAIN
65. Palabra de Vida, Madrid
66. El Señorío de Jesús, Vitoria

PORTUGAL
67. Comunidade A Boa Nova, Lisbon

TURKEY
68. Temple of the Holy Spirit, Istanbul

LEBANON
69. Illuminator's Lamp, Beirut
70. People of God Community, Beirut, with branches in Kuwait, Qatar, and the United Arab Emirates

SYRIA
71. Emmanuel Community, Aleppo

ISRAEL
72. Jesus Is Alive, Haifa

INDIA
73. Community of the Good Shepherd, Vasai
74. Community of Jesus: Light of the World, Mumbai
75. Krist Kiran Parivar, Pune
76. People of Praise, Bangalore
77. Community of the Risen Lord, Borivali

Intergenerational Community

The vision of intergenerational community is a challenge to achieve, and that challenge has greatly increased with the growth of a globalized, media-driven youth culture.

In the earliest years, the challenge was manifold. We were learning about family life and raising children in the midst of a culture in which family life itself was being challenged in an unprecedented way.

In spite of this, the communities persevered and beginning in the 1980s a major effort was made to understand the needs and challenges and respond to them. Slowly these efforts bore fruit. As time has gone on, a greater percentage of children raised in community are making an adult choice to embrace the call to covenant community life.

The Gap program, in which young people go to live and serve in other communities, was established in 1996 in Monterrey, Mexico. In this way, youth could experience the richness of life in a multi-national, intercultural community.

Your eyes will weep at what you see, your ears will tingle at what you hear and your hearts will leap for joy at the surprising things I am about to bring to you.
For I say to you that I am about to open to you a new age of evangelism among young people, the likes of which you have not seen.
What I have done here and there among you I will now do abundantly in your midst.
Prepare yourselves for an intake of young people that is beyond your capacity to handle. Prepare yourselves, for you lack the resources.
Pray that I provide you the resources to receive, not growth, but multiplication.

A profound challenge for the Sword of the Spirit will come in the decade of the 2020s when the majority of the founding generation—those men and women who came of age before 1980—reach retirement age and withdraw from leadership.

For fifty years, the vision of Christian community, empowered by the action of the Holy Spirit and bound by covenant commitment, has persisted in the Sword of the Spirit and in other covenant communities throughout the world and has had effects well beyond the communities themselves. If this call and mission are to continue, a new generation must take up this vision and persevere in the work that their elders, with the help of the Lord, labored in the Spirit to accomplish.

Kairos

While the various Sword of the Spirit outreaches to young people have their own name and identity and need to be suited to their own circumstances and challenges, they use many of the same methods and share the same basic goals.

As these outreaches have developed, the leaders in the various communities have sought ways of sharing these lessons and other resources across the Sword of the Spirit.

In 1995, outreach leaders in North America set up a program available to all the communities in the region called the Regional Youth Program, later called Christian Youth Challenge.

This regional youth program aimed to draw on existing programs and resources to encourage young people who grew up in community to come into a personal relationship with Christ and to embrace the vision of Christian community for themselves.

Other regions of the Sword of the Spirit began similar programs, and discussions among the leaders of these programs led to fruitful cooperation.

More and more young people, generally of university age, began to visit communities in other regions, sometimes for extended periods.

In January 2007, the various regional youth programs adopted the common name **Kairos.**

While some local groups have adopted this as a name, most of the groups united under the Kairos banner have retained their own names and missions.

By coordinating plans for youth programs from childhood to early adulthood, Kairos seeks to implement the vision of the "youth bridge," a comprehensive approach that guides young people through the various stages of development, to help them grow into mature disciples.

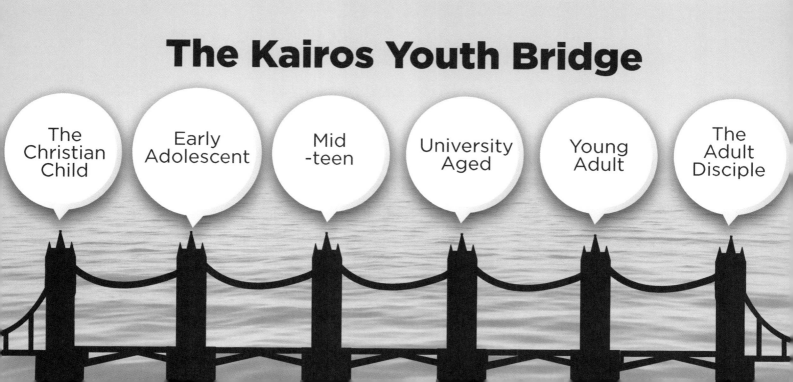

The Kairos Youth Bridge

The Christian Child

Early Adolescent

Mid-teen

University Aged

Young Adult

The Adult Disciple

Outreach to Youth

Detroit Community Outreach - Youthworks Detroit

The outreach in Detroit began in 1995 with a summer program started by two Servants of the Word brothers, Dave O'Connor and Stan Mathay, who were teaching at a charter school in Detroit sponsored by several local Protestant churches and by the Catholic Archdiocese of Detroit. This summer program, later called Youthworks Detroit, drew on young volunteers, initially from UCO chapters, who came to the city to work with the poor and particularly with young people.

A household of Servants of the Word, a family from the Word of Life community, and a household of single men moved to Detroit in 2000. The purpose was not directly to build a Sword of the Spirit community in Detroit, but through our community presence in Detroit to work with local Christian churches and other groups to help the people of the city in whatever way we could.

Detroit has become a favorite destination for young people from communities in the United States and throughout the Sword of the Spirit. The summer programs attract dozens of volunteers to work with young people on renovation projects and to engage in direct aid to the poor. Others have moved to Detroit to live year-round and even for the longer term. Both single people and families have moved to Detroit for work or education, creating a cell of community there, linked to the Word of Life community in Ann Arbor.

Youth Initiatives – United Kingdom

Outreach to youth in their teenage years has taken many forms in the Sword of the Spirit. One that has been fruitful in a very challenging environment is Youth Initiatives (YI), an outreach of Charis community in Belfast, Northern Ireland.

Like the community from which it arose, YI is an ecumenical outreach. Youth Initiatives runs a wide variety of programs for youth from eleven to nineteen years of age such as jobs training, after-school activities, and summer camps.

An ecumenical group of young Christians in Northern Ireland is a miraculous phenomenon. As one young participant observed speaking of a YI social gathering.

"Look at this, a real miracle. People from all over Belfast, Catholics, Protestants, different social backgrounds, yet I consider them all my family"

University Outreach

Many communities in the Sword of the Spirit had their origins on university campuses. It is not surprising, then, that outreach among university students has been a regular part of life in many of our communities. These university outreaches go by many names but they follow a similar pattern: to proclaim the Gospel, to help people encounter the person of Jesus Christ in the power of the Holy Spirit, and to form young people to become missionary disciples.

In many communities, the university outreaches go by the name of University Christian Outreach (UCO), but many others have their own distinctive names:
Cristianos en Marcha (Christians on the Move), Árbol de Vida community in San José, Costa Rica; Christ's Youth in Action in the Philippines; Misión Católica Universitaria (University Catholic Mission) in Monterrey, Mexico; and St. Paul's Outreach (SPO), a Catholic university outreach originating from Christ the Redeemer Community in St. Paul Minnesota (USA), now with multiple chapters throughout North America.

Today, our university outreach programs—by whatever name—carry on our call and mission in the Sword of the Spirit by raising up zealous young men and women as disciples of Jesus Christ, to strengthen and extend our communities and to serve the mission of the Christian people throughout the world.